A MOMENT OF SILENCE

Henry Smith

A Moment of Silence
Copyright © 2019 by Henry Smith

Tellwell Talent

www.tellwell.ca

ISBN

978-0-2288-0971-5 (Paperback)

978-0-2288-0972-2 (eBook)

TABLE OF CONTENTS

ACKNOWLEDGEMENTS

There are times when silence speaks so much more loudly than words of praise to only as good as belittle a person, whose words do not express, but only put a veneer over true feelings, which are gratitude at this point of time.

To my work book editor and interior designer, Sally, James and Elliot my Project Manager, thanks for taking the time to lay this out and providing me the inspiration to do this, I appreciate you more than you'll ever know!

To some of the important people; Corine Hester, Dana Wright, Vanessa Lee, Nancy Stith, and all others who took the time to help me find some needed corrections to the original book that only made this work book even better.

It has been my pleasure to work with terrific people at Tellwell talent, and to those who have been courteous and efficient and have taken a genuine interest in this book.

CHILD MOLESTATION

I can say with some authority that no one should take an ounce of joy in these revelations and accusations. This is not a political issue, even if people, including abusers themselves, have hypocritically used it as one.

This is not the time for giddiness or gloating. Child sexual abuse is tragic and traumatic for its survivors, and that is where the bulk of the focus should always be.

When a child is sexually molested or sexual abused, it breaks bonds of trust. It is a violation of the sovereignty of self and one's zone of physical intimacy. It is an action of developmental exploitation, and it is a spiritual act of violence that attacks not only the body but also the mind.

***

This book contains the experience and observations I have gained over many years as a hearing-impaired parent. My hope is to share these experiences and observations with you.

At three years old I became hearing impaired. The reason why is still unknown; however, no one in my family is deaf! Why me? I could hear and speak once, but everything just faded away.

For years I have lived in a world of silence. For the past fifteen years I have walked around with the idea of putting memories of my past on paper. The changes that occurred during my lifetime are immense. My childhood experiences are so different from what I experience now, of course. The question is: What in my past stopped me from proceeding now? I have an occasion to present these memories. I have asked for some assistance, but no one was there for me. I have included my daughter's memories in their own words, but sometimes memories are just blended with others. Now I'm alone on this journey called independence. I believe that as long as I have my sense of humor, I can make it through and handle what life has offered me.

I love my heavenly Father so much. Without him I am nothing, and I believe that your faith is very important. Without it everything will fall apart. I can't explain what happened to me in my childhood. Read about my life, and tell me what you think.

CHAPTER 1

A MOMENT OF SILENCE

I remember this dream so vividly, from the first moment I was taken up. At the moment of my transition, I discovered something amazing. For the first time I had the impression that this required looking at it a different way—in other words, going along with the meaning of what unfolded before me. It was no longer a matter of being but rather a kind of attentive biography in play. I don't know how to explain it. All of a sudden, I understood that every movement had a meaning, and it meant something other than itself.

This was an incredible sensation, and it frightened me because I felt charged with a very important obligation: to do it well, because it was extremely important and because I was chosen. I felt I understood everything the angels understood, and I began to understand their questions.

It's been an interesting journey living in a world of silence, along with my life as an independent mother in this ever-changing society. Over the years I have matured. I can't explain what happened to me when I was younger. Read about my life, and tell me what you think.

For years I have lived in a world of silence. For the past fifteen years I have walked around with the idea of putting memories of my past on paper. The changes that occurred in my lifetime are immense. My childhood experiences are so different from what I experience now, of course. The question is: Who might be interested in my past? I have an occasion to present these memories. I have asked for some assistance, but no one was there for me. I have included my daughter's memory, but sometimes her memories are just blended within. However, now I'm alone on this journey called independence. I believe that as long as I have my sense of humor, I can make it through and handle what life has offered me. I love my God, and I believe that faith is very important. Without it everything will fall apart.

Welcome to my world. Here you will find everything—well, almost everything—there is to know about me through this biography, which describes the hardships I've endured in my life. Writing and reading is my passion.

I was born March 28, 1967, in Newport News, Virginia, where my mother, Sandy Johnson; my dad, Patrick A. Johnson Jr.; my sister, Louise Johnson, and I lived in a comfortable two-family home.

My father named me Sue, and my mother chose Beatrice as my middle name. I didn't like "Sue" so I chose "Tammy."

My father married my mother on May 30, 1965, after his first wife passed. My dad stood a full foot taller than my mom. He was six foot one, lean, and a handsome man, and he was always in a good mood from the moment he woke up in the morning, full of humor and jokes. In his life he always saw the bright side. My mother was the opposite. She saw things realistically. They were a good couple.

My father was an army veteran, a letter carrier for the postal service, and a car salesman. He was a hardworking, fun-loving man who was an integral part of our family. He loved playing golf with friends.

My dad's first wife died of cancer. My mom knew he had children with his first wife. I found out later that I have three half siblings:

Mary, Paul, and Barry. My relationship with my siblings is good, and in some ways I think it's actually better than my relationship with my birth sister, Louise. We both tend to keep out of each other's way.

Sadly, my father died March 17, 1994, at the age of fifty-two of a massive heart attack. I cried every night in bed. He was my best friend. I miss him very much. I wish I had spent more time with him as I grew older. We had some good times together when he was here, and that's what I think about now.

Many times I wish my mom knew how to speak sign language. While growing up, I never did ask my mother or father how the two met because neither one of them would understand if I asked. As I got older my mom finally said she met my father in Newsome Park area. I had more questions. Did he send her flowers? Did he ask my mother if she had a boyfriend or if she was married? I just wanted to know how it all began, but I never did get around to asking. I do know that my father graduated from Carver High School in Newport News; yes, he was a Trojan. After my father graduated, he went into the military. After the war, he returned home and became a letter carrier for the Postal Service and an auto salesperson. Later, he married my mother and bought a house on 49th Street. I remember when I was only seven years old, all I did was sit in my room and watch television because we had just moved into our home. My bedroom walls were painted yellow and brown. I'll never forget those ugly colors, but I was comfortable. Those are just a few of the things I remember.

I can remember vividly when I was five years old, every summer when school was closed my mom packed my clothes to stay with my grandma. Being with her I had nothing but fun. I used to run up and down the hill with all my cousins. There were six or seven of us. I can say I was pretty fast runner for my age. My cousins couldn't beat me or catch me. The hill was the road that leads out to the highway. My grandmother's house was the only house that sat on top of the hill. It was all alone. As I stood on the hill, one particular day, I recall gazing over their property and saying to myself, "My grandparents own so much land." They had chickens, turkeys, roosters, ducks, and a dog. I guess you would say actually they had a mixture of almost everything. Oh yes, they had one horse too. I don't remember whether they had goats and pigs, but I do remember they had a lake in the back of the house that no one was allowed to go near.

In my grandmother's house there was plenty food to go around, and always after dinner my cousins and I passed our free time by playing card games.

My cousins played with the animals. I was too scared. I wouldn't take any chances getting too close to those animals. I knew if I had gotten closer to those mean roosters, they would chase after me, and I would have been screaming for mercy. It would have been devastating to see these two-legged birds chasing after me up and down those hills, while all my cousins laughed at me.

My grandmother stood just over five feet tall and weighed less than 180 pounds. She was bright, intense, aggressive, and beautiful. She had a great laugh whenever someone said or did something that was humorous.

For years my grandmother was full of anger and disappointment because my mother wasn't always there for me.

After I was born, my parents were incredibly conscientious about me. They loved me very much, but what was really sad was that they had more love for me than for each other. I believe my mother loved my father, but my father was an entirely different case concerning my mother. I was unaware of all this at that time. I just knew I was loved, and I was never shielded from them. I have had a lot of sorrow, but who hasn't at my age? I have played the clown a lot too, but I was hardly conscious of it. I felt lonely but hardly ever in despair! I ought to be deeply ashamed of myself, and indeed I am.

What is done cannot be undone, but one can prevent it happening again. I want to start from the beginning again. It can be difficult. Now that I have my husband, Raymond, to support me, I can and I will make him happy.

I have one outstanding trait in my character, which must strike anyone who knows me for any length of time, and that is my knowledge of myself. I can watch myself and my actions, just like an outsider. For Pam, my autistic daughter, every day I face prejudice without making excuses for her and watch what's good and what's bad about her. I remember so many things about myself that I condemn. I couldn't begin to name them all. I understand more and more Raymond's words were when he said, "All mothers must look after their own upbringing. You can only give a child good advice or put them on the right path, but the final forming of a person's character lies in their own hands."

In addition to this, I have lots of courage. I always feel so strong and as if I can bear a great deal. I feel so free and so young! I was glad when I first realized it because I don't think I shall easily bow down before the blows that inevitably come to everyone. But I've talked about these things so often before now I want to come to the chapter of my dad and mother, who don't understand me.

My father has always thoroughly spoiled me. He was sweet to me, defended me, and has done all that a father could do. And yet I still felt so terribly lonely for a long time. I felt so left out, neglected, and misunderstood. My mother tried all she could to check my rebellious spirit, but it was no use. I have cured myself by seeing for myself what was wrong in my behavior and keeping it before my eyes. How is it that my mother was never any support to me in my hearing impairment struggle? Why did she completely miss the mark when she never wanted to offer me a helping hand? The greatest hand my mother could offer me would be if she only knew how to speak sign language. She tried the wrong methods. She always talked to me as a child who was going through difficult phases. It sounds crazy because she's the only one who has always taken me into her confidence, despite the obstacles we both face. No one but her has given me the feeling that I'm senseless. But there's one thing she's omitted: you see she hasn't realized that for me the fight to get on top was more important than all else. I didn't want to hear about any "symptom of my disability" or my age. I wanted to be treated like a young lady like all others. But my sister, Louise, has her own merits. My family didn't understand me, for that matter. I can't confide in anyone unless a family member tells me about their experience in life.

I don't feel that I can be intimate with my sister because she's always taken up the motherly attitude and never has allowed me to voice my opinion about family matters. She often tells me that she too has had similar passing tendencies, and that's why she performs the way she does. But still she's not able to feel intimate with me like a sister or friend, no matter how hard she tries. These things have made me never mention my views on life, nor I will consider sharing my theories with anyone but my book and my husband, Raymond. I concealed from my mother and sister everything that perturbed me. I never shared my ideals with them because they were never interested. I was aware of the fact that they were pushing me away from them. I couldn't do anything else. I have acted entirely according to my feelings, but I have acted in the way that was best for my peace of mind.

My family never wanted me to marry Raymond because he was much older than me, and for some reason they didn't like him. However, in advance Raymond and I talked about the most private things. My greatest disappointment was I had to make a choice: my mother or Raymond. I chose someone who will be with me for the rest of my life, who loves me and my daughter I know very well that I conquered her instead of her conquering me. I created an image of him in my mind, pictured him as a quiet, sensitive, lovable man who needed affection and friendship. I needed a loving person to whom I could pour out my heart; I wanted a friend who'd help put me on the right road.

I achieved what I wanted, and slowly but surely I drew him toward me. Finally, when I had made him feel friendly, it automatically developed into an intimacy, which, on second thought, I'm glad I allowed. I still don't know quite what to make of my mother. Is she superficial, or does she still feel shame about me? But I committed one error in my desire to make a real friendship: I switched over and tried to get Raymond by developing it into a more intimate relationship, whereas I should have explored all other possibilities. He longs to be loved, and I can see that he's beginning to be more and more in love with me.

CHAPTER 2

MY GRANDMA AND GRANDPA

My grandmother was born in Richmond, Virginia, on June 21, 1922, and passed away on Monday, November 18, 2011. She was my mother's mother. My sweet grandmother Bea was ninety years old. She lived a long life. She had a great sense of humor that was wonderful, but saying goodbye to her was one of the hardest things I've ever had to do. She married my grandfather, Mr. Lewis E. Johnson, in 1939. They lived in Richmond and had six children before their deaths.

My grandpa was a musician and a hard worker, and a family-oriented man. His life may have been full of joy and happiness, but he had to work for it. My grandpa was a man built for others and always put his family and faith above everything else. Every Sunday we looked forward going to church as a family, and it brought us all closer together. This is another aspect of life where Church influenced me. For that I am grateful. Although my grandpa was a regular guy and didn't wear any special costume or have any supernatural abilities, he was powerful and influential to me. I told my grandpa that he was my hero. I wrote it on a piece of paper and gave to him. He read it and smiled and comforted me with a big hug.

My fondest memory was when my grandpa walked me to my bus stop every morning and waited for me there after school. After school we would go out to his favorite restaurant. He would order French fries and all I wanted was ice cream. There were hot summer days. My grandpa and were are best friends. Everywhere he went, I went. We were like twins.

My grandparents raised me because my parents were too busy to look after me. Grandma and I shared a stronger bond than I had with my parents, who I saw only during the weekends and summer. Sometimes I didn't see them at all.

The saddest day was when I lost my grandpa. That was devastating for me. He died May 4, 1972. My family found him lying on the kitchen floor. His heart had stopped. I saw him lying there. I couldn't help myself from crying so much. I cried until my eyes were red. I was only six years old when he passed away. Randomly through the night I would cry because of it. I finally got over it as days and weeks went by. From that day until now I regret not saying goodbye to my grandpa. I always remember one thing. My grandpa loved me, and I know he wouldn't want me to be sad because of his death. He would want me to continue on with my life journey and make out the best I can.

I believe my grandmother was the oldest girl in her immediate family, and well-educated. She became a nurse's aide, and she made a difference in all our lives. She was a nurse for twenty-three years.

My childhood memory is smelling breakfast up on the mountaintop of the hills of Virginia near the woods, where my grandmother lived. Every Saturday morning my grandmother, known to everyone as "Mother Bea," would be up around 4:00 a.m. preparing an old-fashioned breakfast. It usually consisted of made-from-scratch pancakes, link and patty sausages, bacon, eggs, toast, and red Kool-Aid. I shared a room with my two cousins April and Michelle, who were with me every summer as a vacation away from Newport News, Virginia.

I remember how Grandma used to ease herself into the kitchen as quiet as a mouse trying not to wake anyone, However, once she entered in the kitchen, I could see her hands reaching for pots and pans above cabinet. Our house friends and family always took the shortcut through Grandma's kitchen; of course, they never used the front door. Everyone always came through the back door that led into Grandma's kitchen. She would cook a large dinner for the entire family. She'd have fried chicken, roast turkey, and biscuits. You could smell the food miles away. My favorite dessert was corn pudding. Grandma used to always have candy hiding in her kitchen drawer that she would sneak to me so the rest of my cousins didn't see. She and I were dedicated to snacks, like chocolate bars. Believe me, we never went hungry. We were fed, and Grandpa was never alone because there was always someone over, playing cards with her.

I spent quality time with my grandma. She was my mom away from Mom, and that's how it always was. My grandma never let me down, but my mother… No comment. She always turned my frowns upside down without being funny and just being Grandma. With my grandma's presence I was always smiling and full of joy. I don't recall too many incidents where my grandma would grumble or complain. I remember her as a peaceful, joyful, and loving person. She was a woman with strong faith in God and great perseverance.

When I was a little girl, I had a head full of thick, long, black hair that had been growing for eight straight years. Every night before I went to sleep, my grandma would take time to brush my hair and put it in long braid. This was another memory of my grandma, the braiding of my hair. Even in the simple things, my grandma was more than willing to set herself aside to help those in need. She was the backbone of strength and stability of our family. Many lessons, morals, and values were learned from her. Soon she had little ability as far as being able to move or walk like she used to. She needed twenty-four-hour assistance, with being in and out of the hospital so often. I once didn't think my grandma was going to make it for my wedding on August 17, 2007. It was the happiest day of my life to see her there. I was excited to see her. My mother wore a beige pantsuit. It was the same color as my wedding gown. I was excited to see my grandma partake in my wedding. She was there to represent me. She was my rock.

I discovered my grandmother was having hard times exercising like before, when she was active. It became difficult for her to do the things she once did. She was a wheelchair. My mother said her blood and heart were abnormal. She rushed my grandma to the hospital unable to breathe. Her doctor gave her an oxygen concentrator. I understood that without her oxygen, she could get Alzheimer's later in life.

Over the years my grandmother had several episodes of hospitalization. Sometimes she would be hospitalized two or three times in one year. However, one particular, unsuspecting day, November 8, 2010, everything came to a complete halt. My mother had called my husband at 4:30 in the morning. I had left for work before she called him to confirm that my grandmother had passed away peacefully. That morning my husband texted me. I immediately turned around and raced home. I rushed to the hospital after being told about the tragic passing. I just walked up to her and wrapped my arms around her still one last time. I laid my head on her chest and kissed her cheeks.

I was the last family member to spend some private final moments with her. I knew that when I left that room I would never see my grandmother again. Earlier, I was sitting in the ER with my grandma, and it was the most comfortable place for me. I said a few more prayers for her. I wished her soul a speedy journey to her next home and that she would be released from the burdens of this life. Her spirit, her fire had already left when I arrived the first time. Initially, when I walked into the room, I did not feel any sort of awareness, energy, or life coming from the room besides that of the nurses. She had gone to heaven.

However, I did have a very strong sense of her being there when I sat there alone with my grandmother. I had blocked out everyone who was sitting around me. But the feeling did not come from her body. It came from an upper corner of the room, and it stayed there the whole time when my husband and I were in the emergency room when the nurse moved her body away. The feeling in that room was gone. It was like her spirit had left her body.

She was my best friend at ninety years old. My grandmother died of heart failure and high blood pressure. In the emergency room I rushed over to her as close as I could. I never wanted to let her go. I wanted a moment alone to be with her. I wanted that moment to last forever. As I grasped her, I thought about what I was going to do without her by my side to cheer me up and protect me if something went wrong in my life. What was I going to do now? Who was going to braid my hair before bed? She had always been there for me, and I wasn't ready for her to leave me. I was terrified and full of sorrow, but that isn't how she wanted me to feel. My sister Louise put her arms around me sobbing, saying in sign language that our grandma was going to be okay. She went to heaven.

I'm so grateful for having someone like my grandma, who loved and understood me just as I am. She gave me love and affection, and comforted me when I was afraid. My love for her will always be deep down in my heart.

I can vividly picture the day before my grandma's death at my mother's house. I was in her room standing at the foot of her bed, with tears streaming down my face. She was physically weak and unable to move on her own. We all knew that this was almost the end, but I knew she wasn't scared because she realized she was on her way to experiencing endless joy and absolutely no pain. I watched her closely as she helplessly lay in her bed, barely able to move her head and open her eyes. My mother informed her that I was standing at the foot of the bed. She obtained enough strength and slowly opened her eyes. She lifted her head and made eye contact with me and smiled a peaceful smile. I kissed her and left her room. That day I had an uneasy feeling that it was going to be the last time I would see her.

I wished I could see her just once more walking through my door, but I knew that was impossible. I read her lips, but not anymore. She's gone. Yet my heart is broken because I can't understand why someone so precious life has to expire so soon. I pray that God will give me strength and somehow get me through as I struggle with this heartache caused by losing her.

In precious memory of Mrs. Betty Bae Johnson, who walked through Heaven's gate November 18, 2011.

CHAPTER 3

RELATIONSHIPS

All I want is love! Someone who really appreciates me is what I longed for. I am a person who is relationship-oriented. So, I kept trying again and again. Not having any romance, to me, is scarier than going through adversity. I can honestly say that I had my share of romantic troubles.

Many women have one thing on their minds: S-E-X. They are having intercourse with someone they don't love. I experienced this for myself. I had my moments.

So many women feel incomplete unless they have a man in their life. **What we wish for is affection, love, and unconditional acceptance in a relationship.** We continue to hope that a relationship lasts a lifetime, but most women look in the wrong places for a man. They search for all of the wrong reasons.

What men do is sweet talk us and tell us lies in order to have sex with us. Accept it. That is one of the games men play to get over. That happened to me more than once. I have experienced poor relationships, and I felt used, hurt, in pain, and rejected. One boyfriend choked me so hard and left a bruise because of jealousy. When my first marriage ended, I found myself hurt and in pain again.

When my marriage ended I took a long hard look at myself. I cried out, "Why? Why me?" Now I have matured to the point that I take full responsibility for my choices. I am able to say, "I have chosen this situation." I screwed it up, and it's my fault! It's easier not to dwell on mistakes when you own them and learn the lesson. When I realized I had the power to change, it was an eye-opening revelation. It gave me a lot of hope.

While sitting in my kitchen at approximately 9:30 a.m., in a blue-and-white Cowboys jersey and sipping hot tea, at age forty, I was able to feel pride within myself again. People still say I look like an exceptionally pretty college student, with my smooth skin, ponytail hanging down my back, and dark brown eyes. I don't speak like the common world does because I have a hearing impairment. I'm still woman enough to speak my words and express myself, even if it's through lip reading and sign language. And when I choose to, I give my voice a Moment of Silence.

Everybody has a right to have secrets. I've been the individual who confesses my past mistakes. Some say it has become something of a trademark for me. I have talked about my tough upbringing, disastrous marriage, and the glories of newfound love. Just before it all headed south yet again, I convinced myself that this time it would be different. I've been working to break old habits and change how I think about relationships for a while. There was a time I couldn't accept what I was doing to myself. I was under the misconception that I needed drama in my personal life. I have a lot of fears and negative thoughts. Those fears became a self-fulfilling prophecy for me. My goal has been to change my focus from "I don't want to be hurt anymore, and I don't want to be cheated on" to "I just want someone honest."

No one can undo what happened in my past. It was all about relationships and trusting family members. My sense of worth was so low, I had to reprogram myself to see the good in me. I promised myself I would never be a coward again, despite my disability. I will stand up and speak up for what is right. I thought justice would end the cycle of bad romantic choices, but it didn't prove quite so easy a task. I did some things over and over, until finally I understood that it's been my path toward breaking destructive patterns.

My relationship with a soldier who was already taken was really horrific. We were deeply involved after one year. I wish I had left him then, but I was putting everyone's needs before mine. Still, I knew this time I had the right to set boundaries and say, "This isn't OK for me." The relationship ended after two years.

My mother, who is a nurse, helped me throughout my life. I must credit her for helping me finally after the course of trouble in my love life. As you get older, you realize you are entitled to the right to feel better. The thing I hated most was being told what to do. I hated the fact that I took bad advice from other people. I hated being left alone.

During my past marriage I noticed that I had begun to develop really good sign language and communication skills. That was a big part of my evolving and learning how to be in the world of silence. I have been so blessed that I feel I no longer have the right to be selfish anymore.

It was July 12, 1986. I was babysitting that day, and my friend Marcia, who I hadn't seen in quite a while, brought a man to my home who I couldn't see in the dark. He wasn't attractive to me at that time. I guess it was because I couldn't see his face in the darkness. The light on the street had been hit and was not working.

Marcia is also a woman of silence. She's deaf. She had a pretty smile on her face, and I knew that was her way of letting me know she had something for me. In sign language she asked me to come to the car. She was full of excitement, like she wanted to show off a gift she had. Yes, it was a gift. It was a stranger, a man I'd never met but came to be happy with as he became an intricate part of my life. He was sitting there waving his hands. "Hello," I said, waving my hands back to him.

It was not long after we met and began hanging out together that he immediately developed a crush on me. I didn't know how he felt then, but he revealed it to me after nineteen years of friendship. We became friends first. Now we are intimate. He was the one I could rely on. He was always there when I needed someone to talk to. He would say all the right things. When I became depressed, he opened my eyes so I could see the light concerning relationships. He showed me just how much others disrespected my life.

I was not attracted to him initially. But all that mattered at that moment was that the man I had started hanging out with and developed a friendship with was married. I trusted him and deemed him worthy of being in my life. His name was Raymond. I only wish he had said something about that when we first met. He never did say anything to me about being married. I remember him asking me, "What are your dreams?"

I told him, "What I deserve most is a perfect love relationship."

I remembered that he quoted to me: "My dreams may come true one day!"

I'm a forty-year-old woman, and yet in my entire life I've felt so unlike most people my age. Dating has never been a problem for me. I am simply not attracted to most people because I'm hearing impaired. At my age and having been a single parent, I just wanted to find someone who would provoke both my heart and a love for my daughter.

Three years ago I ran into Raymond again, at a funeral. Actually, we hadn't seen each other in over six years, but we had communicated through text. I've never been on the whole long-distance relationship scene because sometimes I consider myself to be hopeless in the world of romance. The idea of loving somebody without being able to be near them is sort of heartbreaking.

My friend Raymond is amazing. He is one of the most intelligent people I've ever met. He is thoughtful, provoking, and inspiring, and we have so much in common. It's kind of scary because years ago we were just friends. Now he's divorced, and we're together. We're engaged and planning to be married. I love this man so much that when he leaves me for work, I am unable to stop thinking about him. There is a sizable age difference. I'm forty and he's fifty-three, but that doesn't stop me from loving him.

We were friends first, and now he's my husband. This was unexpected. In fact, I never thought this would happen. When we were friends, I looked at Raymond once in a sexual moment because I was lonely. I wanted him to fulfill my needs, but to no avail, because he was married at the time. When I tell friends about our nineteen years of friendship without any intercourse, they find it unbelievable. We are proof that a man and a woman can be friends and not be intimately involved. He and I just hang out a lot because I feel comfortable being around him. I trust him, and he protects me from those who try to abuse me verbally, mentally, and physically. He is different from all of the men I have ever met. He respects me, and I like that in a man. Friendships develop from mutual respect. When a relationship is built on mutual, authentic friendship and not lust, it has a much better chance of going the distance.

I know my husband is a good man because he took care of his mother. He will do the same for me. He invited me to meet his mother, who is deaf and blind. I will never forget when I first walked into his mother's apartment. She was sitting there asleep in her favorite chair. My husband woke her up with just a touch. I had never seen a person who was deaf and blind. I was excited to see how he communicated with his mother, as they exchanged sign language. And when she did sign language, I understood very little of what she was trying to say. I noticed her sign language was different from what I know. That showed me that even though we both lived in a world of silence, we were equally blessed to have someone like my husband, who loved us and was able to communicate with us in a way we both understood individually.

CHAPTER 4

I REFUSE TO THINK OF MY PAST

Let's say I messed up big time with past relationships. Actually, I made all the wrong moves! I lost my self-esteem and virginity in the process. I'm ashamed of my actions. I'm filled with guilt. I have been struggling mentally, physically, and financially while dealing with my past failures. It seems that I can't move forward. I made a choice that was totally unacceptable.

I refuse to live in my past, however. I had to pray to God and ask His forgiveness so that my mind and my thoughts would be free. I allow myself to cling to hope. God can still use me. He still has plans for me and my newborn child. It will be over soon; I will forget my mistakes and learn from them. And remember: the devil is our adversary. He loves nothing more than for you to wallow in self-pity and for you to lick all your blisters. Your mind and thoughts have been tampered with when you didn't know your own fate.

I will never forget that dark season in my life. There were nights when I did not want to go to sleep. My mind dwelled on how devastated I was. I was embarrassed and greatly humiliated by someone

I loved while carrying my firstborn. Someone with whom I brought a life into the world, I believed loved me. I was so sure the relationship we had was perfect.

What mother wouldn't want a family with the one she so deeply loved? "You have messed up big time" is what I kept hearing over and over and over in my mind. I knew these thoughts were none of mine, but Satan's. I said to myself, "Eventually I can forgive you, but not today." I cannot and will not forget how I suffered with a broken heart and how I was so full of anger. My mind was tormented by the fact that I was trapped.

I had to stay focused because God had work for me to do. He's the only judge who knows all of the facts. My heartbreak did not catch Him by surprise. He knows that "all things work together for good, to those who love Him" and believe in Him. I love the Lord with all my heart. I take His words and feed my spirit with them so that I can become stronger than ever. I hide His words in my heart and ask Him for forgiveness and for Him to renew my mind.

I began to observe my interpreter, who speaks sign language. He was telling me what my pastor was saying. He said, "God wants to help me through this ordeal." I was told to put my differences and feelings aside. So I tried to put everything in the right perspective, of course.

I did not come to see this side of me until my firstborn left me. I was determined to make my life as near perfect as I could. Prayerfully, I took into consideration what my pastor told me. I stopped worrying about my reputation and began to place my focus on my Christian walk. I had temporarily lost focus on God, but now I am free! I share this experience with you to encourage my firstborn that God can use whatever you offer up to Him if you offer it with faith and love.

As I sat in church one particular Sunday morning, I began to think and recollect when I was going through my ordeal and how God spoke to me. It was and is His desire that I bring my troubles to Him and leave them at the foot of the cross. The Lord said, "That's why He died—for every pain, every disappointment, every sinful act done in the past, present, and future."

It was right then that I offered up to Him everything I had been holding on to that was not of Him or for my best interest. I was immediately set free and cleansed. That drama from depression was no longer with me. I was no longer handicapped by my past. I had given it all to my Redeemer, the Savior of the entire world.

You can do the same. He is no respecter of persons. I had every reason to be depressed for the rest of my life, but instead I chose to cry out to God for forgiveness, and He forgave me and cleansed me of all unrighteousness. He promised to do the same for you when you sincerely seek Him. I may not forget your mistakes, but God does not hold them against us. However, we must face the consequences as a result of our disobedience. It is true; we do reap what we sow. When God forgives us, we are forgiven forever! That is why it is so important to maintain an attitude of humility and to own up to your sins or mistakes. Open your heart to God, not to me. He is the only one capable of renewing your mind and making you brand-new. It is how you serve Him after He has forgiven you that matters most.

This chapter is dedicated to my firstborn.

CHAPTER 5

LIFE EXPECTANCY

Since birth I have had a profound hearing loss, which means I have a 90 percent loss of my ability to hear. That's a greater loss than the average hearing-impaired individual. I wasn't born this way. By definition the term "hearing impaired" does not necessarily mean completely deaf. Not all hearing impaired are 100 percent deaf. It is worth noting that some people think "hearing impaired" is the equivalent of the word *deaf*. Many people are politically incorrect in that assumption. Also, in other countries and in some deaf communities, the word *deaf* is full accepted and is actually preferred over the phrase *hearing impairment*.

I can't talk, but I can read lips. I am also a very fast typist. I speak sign language. Since my parents decided to concentrate on teaching me to talk, we used lip reading and finger spelling.

Right after high school, my father wanted to send me to Gallaudet University. I wanted to become a model, but my mother refused to accept that career choice for me. Needless to say, that was one of my dreams, as well as being with my peers as a student.

Yes, I'm different. I consider myself to be special. I say this about myself without conceit but with confidence and appreciation for all things that are beautiful. I like to laugh. I like to joke a lot. I enjoy showing people who I am. I'm a very fun-loving person. I like taking risks at the expense of being adventurous. I like things that are cool, like rims on a car. I hate the typical because that bores me. I like to go bowling. I love going to the movies. That's just who I am.

Once I got rebellious and decided I was going to do my own thing, and I did just that. Enjoying whatever I do is most important to me. I love joking all day long with my coworkers. It's fun because I am blessed with great personalities around me. It is a delight being in the presence of people who enjoy my company and those with whom you don't have to worry about drama.

Concerning my hearing, the higher the frequency of the sound, the louder the sound has to be in order for me to hear it. I require about eighty decibels to be able to hear the sound of beautiful music. A decibel is "a unit used to express relative difference in power," says the *Second College Edition of the American Heritage Dictionary*. To help me hear better, I wear my behind-the-ear hearing aids. This enables me to hear sounds as quiet as forty decibels, which is about the same volume as a newspaper rustling a just a few feet away in a quiet room. However, that does not allow me to hear high sounds above my hearing impairment.

The way it works is I can hear music if the volume is turned up to a certain limit. People ask me, "How do you speak in a silent world alone?" I tell them I can lip read and speak but not clearly. At my level of hearing loss, it is very difficult for me to follow people when they are speaking too quickly. It is nearly impossible for me to keep up. A good example is a teacher who is giving a lecture. He or she moves around and doesn't face me. They talk too fast or are too far away for me to lip read. Another problem is that some words look the same on the lips and also sound almost exactly the same. Sometimes it is difficult for me to hear the difference between the words like *cat, net,* and *bat.*

The things that make speech communication easier for me are bright lighting and a person speaking facing me directly. Please don't move your head around. When you are communicating, maintain your distance from me between two and three meters. Talk slowly, preferably one phrase at a time. Sometimes it is easier for some people to use a notepad or keyboard to communicate with me. If you have chatted with other people by text or email, through typing you will find it very easy to communicate. Email is an ideal means of communicating with me.

It seems technology had advanced just for me. Now there are many possible ways to communicate with other people. We refer to on as "over the line," such as TTY (text telephone) or TDD.

When I was younger, I can remember vividly how my mother always played favorites between me and my sister. She made it painfully obvious that she disapproved of me and my ideas. This had been going on since I was a child. Maybe it was because I was hearing impaired. I admit, I was different, but now I am forty-one years old. I have made numerous attempts to win the love of my mother but to no avail.

Once, my mother forgot my birthday. I was shocked and disappointed. This was before I married my husband. There were jabs at my husband and me for not having a plan for my life. It really bothered me.

My sister had the audacity to call my husband an old man at my wedding. She did that intentionally in front of our guests. It was not the appropriate thing for her to say to him. I wanted to tell her and my mother that I won't take their abuse any longer. But I thought it would be a cruel thing for me to do, to tell them off and express exactly how I felt, on my wedding day. That was supposed to be one of the happiest days of my life. My family will have to accept the fact sooner or later that I know what is best for me. I've been given the gift of my husband, who loves me, and I will be grateful for him being in my life for the rest of my days. No one's attitudes and comments will rain on my parade—my choice, my blessing from heaven.

CHAPTER 6

HOW CAN A RELATIVE BE SO CRUEL?

Before I begin telling my story, I would like to take this time to thank you, my readers, for reading my story. I need to warn you: this is not to hurt anyone. This is to help people like myself who have been through what I endured in the past as a child. This was nasty. I want to help those who might be going through the same things I have gone through and still am going through. I have not yet told my family about it. I have been able to tell only my husband. The reason it took so long to talk about it with my husband was because of fear. I couldn't bear the thought of hurting him with the details of my abuse. He knew a little and knew something bad had happened to me but not as much as what really took place. Luckily he is a very understanding and caring man. He loves me no matter what happened in the past. He has been a big help in my healing, and I have been able to be very honest with him about my feelings in the past.

I have yet to get help from a therapist. I have only recently been able to talk about this. I am forty-five-years old now. I thought I had put this all behind me. And I thought I was able to deal with it. But I was wrong! It wasn't until after I started having children of my own that I saw the innocence of a child.

I am a victim of molestation. Now I'm ready to direct you into another journey. Yes, as a child I was sexually assaulted. I had to find the courage inside myself to escape my fate. I had to face my fears and deal with my emotions. My childhood with my disability was very stimulating. There are so many of us with disabilities who have endured abuse by the very people in charge of protecting us and keeping us safe from harm's way. Now I find out they are the ones who left me with this devastating memory, and they are the very people who hurt and harmed us the most. I had to trust them because my family trusted them.

My childhood innocence was robbed at seven or eight years old. At such a young age I can recall countless memories of what happened and how.

I lived through some pretty horrific abuse at the hands of experienced boyfriends but not as horrific as some. Perhaps more horrific than others, but I won't minimize what I lived through. It was hell, pure and simple. I was overwhelmingly affected, and in my view, that is the measure of hell.

The earliest I can remember when all the sexual abuse started for me as a youngster was by a family member. The hardest part about this was they were in control of what we did, but as time went on, it progressed. They would make me do things to them that I knew I didn't like. This went on for years. This is very hard for me to write about, but I feel it has to be told.

I remember him making me perform on him, and he was masturbating in front of me and making me watch. He wanted me to do the same in front of him or have us do this together at the same time. I can remember screaming out, and he would laugh. The pain was so devastating. It felt as though a knife had just stabbed me, but still he took it further. I was thirteen years old when he tried to sleep with me all night in my bed. I can remember feeling so sick to my stomach. I felt so gross! I never told anyone because I was scared. I always felt I was to blame, just as much as he was. However, to be honest, I was ashamed and confused with guilt.

The person who did this to me wasn't the only one who abused me along the way. There were other family members who preyed on me because of my disability. I was an easy target because I couldn't talk or tell what was going on.

There was a neighbor of my grandmother's. I always knew her growing up as being so kind. But one day I was sitting on her front porch with her like we always did, and nothing ever happened. But one day she started touching me. I was about ten years old, I guess. She started out grabbing at my breast while my grandma was at work. She was supposed to watch over me until my grandmother got off. She would tease me about how large my breasts were. Of course, they were only so large as I was only ten years old. Again as an abused child, this was the way it was. I became so adapted to them coming on to me and touching me that I allowed it to happen. I can remember going into her house and being taken upstairs. I can remember the day cigarette smoke was coming from this woman's body and breath. She would lay me down on her bed, fondling me. To this day I get sick to my stomach every time I think of her. I never told my grandmother. What's the use? No one would ever do anything about it anyway.

I can remember going home, climbing into my bed, curling up in the fetal position and crying! Asking, "Why me?"

There were many men and women after me. They tried to come on to me in some way or made me feel very uncomfortable. But never again did a man or woman ever put hands on me or abuse me anymore.

I had to write my story because I want my victories to shine through. Not just my memories but my victories that I have achieved my own path to healing and recovery from what I experienced. I want other survivors who are wracked with guilt and shame to know that it's not their fault. I know people with disabilities often believe it is their fault. I also believed I was to blame because I believed the lies I had been told. But I got help, and with that help I was able to let go of all the lies I had come to believe.

I want all the survivors of visual impairment, deafness, and hearing impairment who are desperately trying to cope with feelings of hopelessness and despair to know they're not alone. I was also stricken with those same hopeless thoughts, even suicidal thoughts. I found who I really was when I got the help I needed. I want all my survivors to know there is hope, real hope. My testament is to that hope.

I have a very loving and caring husband! I couldn't imagine life without him. He is the kindest and most caring gentleman I know. He has never hurt me in any way! Has never laid a hand on me in anger or ever called me bad names. I'm just sorry it took me so long to come to him with all this. Now that he knows, I can move on. I have not yet told my mother about the abuse that took place. I don't feel as though I can. I'm not even sure if I ever will be able to. Right now I just need to concentrate on me and get the help I need from my Lord and Savior Jesus Christ and move on with my life.

Thank you so much for reading my story. It was very hard for me to write all this down. I just hope it has helped someone who has been through what I have been through. You are not alone! It was not your fault, and it's OK to tell it now.

My life with my disability, I'm here on this earth to show the world and my community that I am somebody. I'm like them. I know I'm different. I'm special and have always felt that way. As a child my family and other people has viewed me as something less due to my disability, but my ex-husband doesn't. He is one of the few people in the world who understand me quite well. He enunciates perfectly so it's easy for me to read his lips.On top of that, he is an extremely aminated person who uses facial and bodily expression.

When I was 4 years old I felt so different because of my disability, unable to hear or speak. I felt that I was all alone,. trapped in another world. I would think there was no one out there like me, but there were. I live on the same planet with different societies, cultures and races, but it doesn't mean I'm any different from anyone else after losing my hearing. I have discovered this unique experience. I never would have thought my hearing loss would be more gradual or non-existent in my life coming to this new world. Though I don't agree with the American dictionary definition of the word world, it's exactly like dropping from a alien planet loaded with people with disabilities.

My ex-espouse says I'm different because I like to do almost everything. I have a lot of interest. I like you was in computers. This is my hobbies. I also like watching football and basketball. My favorite teams are the Los Angeles Laker and the Dallas Cowboys. I like reading music writing and also learning new things that my spouse shared with me. I can always get help from my husband, and I'm happy to be his spouse. Listening to music is also problematic in that I invariably cannot Make Out lyrics even though I can not hear words being sung. I prefer jazz music over music with lyrics. But that is not to say that I don't enjoy music I play my CDs everywhere I travel. But the only problem I have is that I can't hear but I can't feel the vibes, I can't hear people speaking clearly but only read their lips, and when I write my grammar is not accurate when I write letters.

CHAPTER 7

DISABILITY VS. CUSTODY: FIGHTING FOR CUSTODY BEHIND THE GATES OF HELL ALONE

I am a self-sufficient, independent woman. A mother who cares about family values, trust, and most of all life. However, I have overcome a lot of obstacles to become who I am today despite my disability. I struggled hard with acceptance when I was a kid, now I have strengthened my faith against my enemies, but in reality it's one of the hardest things to do in life. How do I accept and take pain when my heart gets broken and my emotions are completely powerless? Every day when I look up to the skies I pray that God guides me in the right path of righteousness.

The most tragic experience in my life was when I nearly lost custody of my daughter in court. I had support and assistance of a counsel, but I still, l almost lost hope in this case. My enemies were biased against me. My ex-husband and I divorced over seventeen years ago and have gone our separate ways. Unfortunately, my daughter and I were still living with ex-in-laws. After I chose to move out, taking my baby with me, I was called unfit to take to care of my daughter because of my disability. My baby was diagnosed in her later years with autism, and when the family and friends found out, no one wanted to babysit her. However, I had surprised everyone when I moved away. There were swift and mixed feelings, and there were threats against me that they were going to take away my daughter if I didn't return her. My baby was just one.

In Newport News Court, I was devastated to know that my eight-year-old daughter Pam was not able to speak or be asked who she'd rather live with. I wrote a note and gave it the attorney: "with her grandmother." After court, my heart turned to scars, which was another fear other than losing my daughter. My coworkers and associates became stigmatized when I temporarily lost custody; they all became silent.

This drama happened so long ago no one ever helped me pick up the pieces that fell to the ground, through many challenges and setbacks. I have learned the importance of holding on and never giving up. The tragedy of losing my friend Marcia has no face, and unfortunately bad things indeed happen to good people. Despite the obstacles, as long as there is breath in my body, there is hope. I hope that deaf people and the hearing impaired will be inspired to never give up fighting for your children. My advice to all mothers who are deaf or hearing impaired is to be strong and never go to court alone.

People seem to be confused everywhere I travel. Sometimes I'm being misjudged and discriminated against because of my disability. No one understands my life, living in a world of pure silence, but it does not stop me from raising my babies. I gave birth at a younger age and married a pretty decent guy (at least, at that time he was my first love), but now there is so much I know that I wish I had known sooner.

I accepted a marriage proposal over eighteen years ago. Now I'm reliant, wise, and well-prepared for the unexpected. I wanted nothing more than a perfect married life. However, after seven years into this marriage, my children and I were deserted. I cried and pleaded for reconciliation to change his heart. I was destroyed with a broken heart. I could not believe he left me and his children to be with someone else; it was totally unexpected. I was honest, and I was a faithful wife. I put my love for him first. I trusted my heart, and I was always open about my feelings with him even if it wasn't good. However, just three months after my divorce, I learned that no one can have a successful marriage unless your soul mate is just as committed to reaching the same journey.

I was divorced in 1994, with only daughter, Pam. Allow me to say it again: upon my divorce I was granted joint custody of Pam, my youngest. Even with everything that's bad about the court system, despite it all I really hoped for justice. All I wanted was equal time with my daughter, who was too young to understand justice. It is my belief that the laws of Virginia concerning child support visitation rights and custody must be changed to bring about fairness and equality. Yes, I am making a statement as a mother for what I believe in. No husband or wife should be granted sole, joint, or full custody of a child when he or she deserts their family. I have no illusions about what justice is, and it happened here in my custody case. My story is very bizarre, and if I was not living this nightmare I'm not sure I would believe it. I remember vividly living in North Carolina when my ex served me the divorce papers. He was in the military. Not only did he file for divorce, but he also filed custody. After I had Pam, it never occurred to me that my ex would initiate this action against me in another state.

I had to reply to his court petition—a North Carolina divorce petition. Now I wish I had stayed in Virginia, not North Carolina.

Being a mother was everything I dreamed of. I never would have believed I was considered expendable in my daughter's life. Before my divorce I was working full time, and my ex was in the military. Both of us were equal parents, but on the very first pretrial motion I was expendable! Even though I lived in his parents' house. After I received the divorce papers, I was depressed. I was afraid to go against a court order. Looking back I wanted to escape and take my babies with me into another country. I never want to let my babies go. I had no idea how corrupt the court system was. I remember my ex spent over $2000 for an attorney who turned out to be a party of taking my babies from me. To my readers, this is just a portion of my story. I believe anyone who reads this book can realize that something is desperately wrong with the family courts in Virginia. Whenever a mother loses all rights to her children when she is not at fault, something is wrong. I have lived through the most barbaric experience. In an instant, my world was shattered when we divorced. Mr. Ex and I will never be free to love or cuddle each other again.

It is outrageous that a family law court in America can rule on divorce and custody and all the while neglect to protect fathers who desert their family. Justice betrayed me and my baby. Justice has deprived their birthrights. I am telling my story for two reasons: because I want others who have had their children or grandchildren unjustly taken to know they are not alone and there are other families who know the pain they live with every day. I also want my daughter know I love her more than anything. I did not abandon you; your father did!

When I moved out of my ex-in-laws' house, I immediately took Pam with me. However, she stayed only two months, but for some reason, she went back to her grandmother's house. Right then I knew I'd lost her. It's not easy dealing with the loss of a person who is dear to you. I had a best friend. She tore me apart, and I feel completely destroyed even now because I never thought anyone could separate us. When I question her, I notice a blank expression on my daughter's face as though someone has been giving her some advice. I had to ask, "What's going on?"

She answered "Nothing." I didn't think my daughter would do what her father did. He deserted Pam and me when he left. I cried. I couldn't hold my emotions. I was stressed. I couldn't sleep at night. I was worried our relationship was much more important and fundamental than my friend Marcia. I'm the only her best friend she will ever have.

CHAPTER 8

SPECIAL MOMENTS

I t's been an interesting journey for me living in a world of silence. In my life as an independent mother in this ever-changing society, I have matured and have seen and experienced some beautiful moments as well as some groundbreaking highs and lows that could have broken my spirit. Somehow I held on because I found strength and hope. Living with my disability I found energy to break down all barriers, and I kept moving forward despite all obstacles I face. I reached my goal.

With a moderately severe hearing loss since three years old, I was given my first pair of hearing aids when I was four years old. At eighteen months I was diagnosed. I'm not deaf; I just have a disability. I've lived for forty years as a person with a hearing aid in a mainstream world. However, it has been a long journey to get where I am today.

I attended a state primary school followed by a community college (Thomas Nelson) with two year of completion of liberal arts, and at thirty-five, I had achieved and participated in events that wouldn't be considered the "norm" for hearing-impaired people. But without the support of friends and other major people who were influential in my life journey, I don't think I would have ever gotten to where I am today.

My hearing impairment is a silent disability, and people still question me about my hearing. Again, I tell them I was born with a hearing disability but during my childhood years began to have a progressive hearing loss that went undetected until I was almost three years old. I learned how to read lips in order to get by. I guess I never knew how bad my hearing loss was because I had learned how to accommodate it from such a young age.

As a hard of hearing person, I can't say I'm bothered when people refer to me as hearing impaired, hard of hearing, or even deaf. All are accurate definitions of my hearing loss, in my opinion.

When I take my hearing aid out, I am pretty much in the dark. The world becomes totally silent. I can't hear voices, the telephone, or the vacuum. I can hear and feel the vibration of a dog bark only if it's in the same room with me, and an occasional loud thump, but that's about it. With my hearing aids in, I can hear voices and follow conversation so long as I can see the faces of the people conversing, relying on reading lips to an extent. The most frustrating is coworkers, friends, and strangers and their misconceptions and attitudes of me. After I tell them I'm hearing impaired, changes occur not only in strangers but also in people within the workplace, family, and acquaintances.

Dealing with stares, receiving unwanted pity, being treated as a child, and having elected officials misunderstand my disability issues are very draining.

As a child through my early twenties I used denial and over-compensation to deal with these situations. During my preschool experience, I was pushed by a teacher to be the best student I could be. I had to work harder in order to prove that I was as good as anyone, even the students without disabilities. I came to believe it was my responsibility to change the attitude that people had toward me.

I always wanted to disprove the perception that people with disabilities, especially those with speech impairment, are slow, friendless, and have no lives. It's funny that even as a small child I knew people had misconceptions about me. I spent hours upon hours doing homework without anyone to help me with my exams. Being the best was my mission. I had to have the top grades. I really had to be number one in everything I did. I also had to be outgoing, funny, and involved in every organization possible. Even after my college years I really thought if I was a good enough person, people would stop staring at me, and society would see me just like any other person.

It was hard. I would always deny the hurt I felt when I was stared at as I shopped around at the mall. At a restaurant I would deny the embarrassment I felt when a waitress would ask my nondisabled friend what I wanted to order. I would deny my feelings countless times in order to press onward in my mission of trying to eliminate the difficult attitudes of people. My thinking was that because I'm hearing impaired, people would think better of me if they thought I had it all together, which meant to never let them see me sweat. Now I have taken my time with my life, and I am learning to accept God-given value I received when I was born. I am a wonderful woman, even with my physical disability. I don't need to use over-compensation and denial to feel good about who I am. The more I truly wrap this way of thinking around my mind, the less of a need I have to change the difficult attitudes found nonunderstanding and prejudice. It doesn't matter if the common "Joe Blow" sees me as a child and then underestimates me. Of course it would be my hope that if he meets me, he will gain disability awareness and see me in a different light.

In today's society I'm able to hold a good job, have a good social life, try to keep fit and healthy, and everything else. I have what is considered a "normal" partner in my husband, which is important to me. People who associate with me enjoy my presence for who

I am, and my disability is a large part of who I am. I am grateful for those people in my life because we all want someone to talk to and family to lean on for support. Hearing impairment is no barrier to me. There may be things I might not be able to do, but I can work around them to be able to do them. When I'm driving, I play my music loud; yes, my music. My hearing is not completely gone, and I have my driver's license. I completed high school, won a couple of work performance awards, and competed at the highest level in a jazz dance, even when I struggled to hear the low-sounding music. I have worked full-time as a stock clerk for Army and Air Force Exchange Service for fifteen years. To work is my choice. There have been some difficult situations in my job like not hearing the forklift behind me. My hearing impairment has had a significant impact, but there has never been a moment in my life when I said I couldn't because of my hearing loss. To be successful I have to be aware of my surroundings. These are the things and processes I have to put in place to be successful.

When a coworker or family member tells me I can't do things because of my hearing impairment, that's like giving me ammunition to prove them wrong and to prove to myself that I can do anything once I put my mind to it. And so far, bearing my goals and objectives in mind, while they have taken some time to achieve, the biggest satisfaction is that I have broken those barriers to achieve them.

Keeping my disability in check, I have achieved what I have in my life. My advice to people who come across someone like myself in the near future: speak normally, and give yourself an opportunity to get to know them as a person. I can somewhat restrict my hearing only when I remove my hearing aid.

I can still do everything a normal person does. Sometimes I have to adjust my situation accordingly. Sometimes I do have bad days, and I get frustrated easily. It's no one's fault but my own. Why? Because of my lack of being able to hear and get out what I'm trying to say because of my loss. My husband has put up with a lot of my own frustration and mood days, but he has given me every opportunity to be myself. He has helped me cope and adjust in everyday situations.

In a moment of silence, I hope and pray a scientific research will come soon and open up my world of silence by talking or listening to deaf or hearing-impaired people like myself. I do have a lot to say. I feel very passionate about our silent world. I will continue to do my part and get involved where I can because I believe I can help make a difference between people being aware and people understanding just how tough some everyday situations are for me and others like me.

CHAPTER 9

I'M NOT STRANGE, I'M JUST DIFFERENT

'm crazy and funny. I make my coworkers laugh. I've always been a humorous person. I'm a sexy person for my husband. I know how to make my husband happy. He's my friend. He's my buddy, and I don't have to do much. He just loves me for who I am. He looks into my eyes and says, "I love you." He's happy with all of me. So I don't have to do anything extra except be married and happy. I love being married to my husband because he's a real man and willing to challenge life with me, and that's what it's all about. I know it's always going to be a little painful, and I don't mean physical pain. I mean mental and spiritual pain.

I often think that other deaf men and women are jealous of me or try to condemn me because of the way I am and how I see life since I have married someone who is not deaf or hearing impaired like myself. I have dated a few deaf men in my life, but I'd rather not anymore because I have experience. They have a lack of romance and affection. None of them ever talked to me about life or what their dreams were in the future. I was never pleased. I needed someone in a different world like myself. I was looking for someone who I could communicate with people around the globe. I needed someone who could deliver messages, someone who could carry on about every day, someone who could carry on conversations and deliver the message that was said back to me in sign language, someone who could hear and speak for me, someone who would assist me in the right path. I'd rather date someone who could love me for me. That's just what I wanted. However, deaf people resent the fact that I only interacted with nondeaf people. I actually lived between two worlds. One world belongs to the nondeaf, and the other world belongs to the hearing impaired. Sometimes I think my deaf associates look at me and say that I've got it made or easy

CHAPTER 10

HEARING IMPAIRED

There are some advantages of being hearing impaired when speaking in sign language. There are over 700 signs in American Sign Language.
Hearing-impaired individuals can

- communicate through windows
- have private conversations in crowded places
- talk to someone in a noisy place without yelling
- talk across a room without shouting
- talk with their mouths full
- talk to someone under water
- express their feelings
- get your attention without disturbing anyone

Learning American Sign Language is a way to bridge the gap between those who can hear and the hearing impaired. It is a beautiful and fascinating language to learn.

There are some disadvantages, with a few listed below.

Hearing-impaired individuals cannot

- call a lawyer for advice
- call police for help
- represent oneself in court
- call a taxicab if they need one
- hear the sound of music or a baby's cry
- order food
- express an illness to doctors and nurses

There are over 20,000,000 Americans who are unable to communicate in sign language.

CHAPTER 11

PAM'S JOURNEY WITH AUTISM

I am going to share a personal story with you about Pam's journey with autism.

Pam was born February 23, 1992, and no, she's not deaf or hearing impaired, only her communication and socialization are her biggest setbacks. I raised my babies on my own for years. Her father abandoned us after she was born. He once denied Pam because of her disability. I felt a mixture of awe, surprise, and disbelief. My daughter understands my sign language well. She also attends Newport Regional Education Centers with her disability. It is a school for autistic students like Pam. She works well with others. She's the most adoring little lady, sweet and so lovable. When Pam was younger, she never tried running out the house or escaping out the front door or climbed out our window. I never have to take the alarm off the wall or secure the window locks. Well, I probably don't have to because she's mature, but she's unpredictable.

Every so often I question whether I am doing enough. These four little words have haunted me since the very moment I received the diagnosis. Not a day has passed that I have not asked myself this question, and every day I feel guilty and fight back my tears as I look at my beautiful daughter and think no, I'm letting my child down. I can't communicate, and I wanted to teach her how to. This guilt has haunted me every day.

Being the mother of a child with autism, I describe my experience with noticing and denying my child had autism, difficulties with communication, getting service, and how the family coped and improved our lives.

I knew something was wrong even before she was a year old. She had many of the warning signs of autism. I think I thought if I denied it long enough, it would go away. Even so, I did realize she needed to be tested for a disability. So at age two I took her in. The fact that she should not communicate made it impossible for testing to occur. For reasons I do not understand, we were told they denied her placement in the public school and in the county preschool for children with disabilities. A few weeks later when she turned three, I had them try again. This time she qualified for preschool for children with disabilities.

At this point she still was not diagnosed with autism, and I was content that she was getting service. But the word *autism* rang through me each time she had a meltdown because she could not communicate with me. She would hit the walls.

As I watched other children in her class who were autistic, I think it slowly crept into my mind that my daughter needed more help. I began to accept that autism was not necessarily a bad thing. The day she started running ahead of me without stopping I knew I had to get her some help. She was diagnosed with high-function autism soon after. Many of the struggles we went through when she was younger are now gone. But with change in age came more struggles. She often has severe meltdowns, sometimes to the point of being violent. Finding a doctor to help manage these autism behaviors was like pulling hair. But when we finally found one, I felt like crying because I knew I could help my daughter. A small dose of medication began to help her impulsiveness, and with the scaled down meltdown, I could then work with her.

Autism has been an unwanted guest in my house for twenty years. It has attached itself to my daughter in a way that I never can. But like so many people I know, I get up and go to battle every day and lie awake strategizing every night.

You see, I was not graced with a baby who came into this world armed with unconditional love for the woman who gave birth to her, fed her, cleaned her, changed her, rocked her, and tried so hard to soothe her. My daughter is autistic, and like any emotion, for her love is a learned task. There is a great deal of heartbreak in this; imagine having to teach your own child how to love you.

Getting my daughter to love me has been like being on an endless job interview. I feel qualified but not confident. I wanted children because I thought I had within me the capability to be a successful mother. I like to think I am loving, nurturing, patient, quick to think on my feet, quick to laugh, and not afraid to work long exhausting hours. However, I'm twenty years into the game, and I still feel years away from knowing if I got the job done.

Sometimes I observe my daughter and ask myself where is the journey going to go for her. My baby is twenty-one years old with the mental capacity of a child. Will my daughter ever get married? I don't know the answer. Will she ever find love? I won't be around forever. I want to know if she's safe. I hope and pray there will be somebody to look after her. I hope she isn't forgotten because I want her to lead a productive life. People ask what autism is. I tell them it's a disorder of brain development, and it affects my daughter's ability to communicate or emotionally connect with people. In some instances, with my daughter having autism, she's totally uncommunicative and unable to care for her most basic needs. She does know how to feed herself. Pam is very independent in that department. My daughter may be autistic, but she's very smart. She has her own private space her room, her TV, and her music. That's all she wants, and if she gets hungry, Pam walks into the kitchen and sits at the dinner table and waits for her meal.

I'm sure that every parent remembers the day their child was diagnosed with autism. For me it was a life-changing moment. My mind was consumed with one thing: fear! It was the fear of what I thought it meant to be autistic. I had never known or even met an autistic person. How in the world was a regular stay-at-home mom like me supposed to have the abilities to raise a child? What would this mean for my precious daughter and for the life of our family? Would my daughter be happy? I had fought so hard to save her. Now I knew I would have to fight equally hard to ensure she had a good life. And so our journey began.

Pam was not born autistic. Things began to change for her at two and a half years old. I never knew if each day would be my last chance to see her. Every trip to the doctor was agonizing, knowing another major complication was right around the corner. However, know surgeries only my daughter back and forth are being unbalance.

My daughter hasn't ruined my life, but autism has ruined her life. Autism has changed our family in many ways, both positive and negative. What stands out overall though is that I will live in dread for the rest of my life as to what her very vulnerable life will be like when we are gone. She will have less money, and there is no way to make sure Pam will be OK. I work hard to not think about what possible horrors she might face from a few family members who just don't give a damn.

I used to lie awake at night wondering why this has happened. There is no family history, and during my pregnancy I ate healthy food. I took prenatal vitamins. But I do know is when my ex-spouse was in the military, he was sent overseas. I do know before he was sent off to war, he was getting adenovirus vaccine shots and influenza vaccination shots, and when he returned back to the United States, he was getting another shot.

Now I have ceased asking why and have surrendered to the fear of where the future will find my child. The fear of thinking who can give her the care and attention that I do if something should happen to me. The pulsating panic I feel when I realize that my life, my future, is as uncertain and unplanned as hers.

To have a daughter with severe autism, I should be out of my mind with stress, but I am more at peace and enjoying life now. I would not change a thing. My husband has taught me unconditional love and compassion. When I do get a moment to myself I know to appreciate it and enjoy it. No moments are ever wasted. Friends told me early on to go with the wave of autism, not to fight against it, and you won't get pummeled and frustrated going with the flow of it a much better ride.

My husband and I have a life, and we know our child is autistic, but it hasn't ruined our lives. Because we say no. Because we look this different path in the eye and say, "OK, this is our life." The future is uncertain for all of us, but we'll deal with it later. Right now I will make accommodations for my daughter and make peace with the fact that my grown-up life is different from what I expected. I will throw every ounce of energy I can into giving her excellent care and a loving home. This is my life, and she's in it, and she has autism. That's the facts, but they're not reason enough to roll over and stop trying.

CHAPTER 12

MY DYSFUNCTIONAL FAMILY

I really believe my mother hates or resents me because I'm not normal like other children. For her to understand me, I wish she knew how to communicate with me in sign language. I'm so lost without her. She resents me. I have believed that for the entirety of my life. There is so much to contribute to this, but I will try to sum it up.

I have my mother, two half brothers, one half sister, one sibling, and two children of my own. I really felt like she has hated me and resented her role of being a mother. My entire life I have witnessed my mom and dad have their differences on what direction I needed to travel because my physical impairment was difficult for them to handle. Growing up, even though I never lied about anything, she still always treated my sister better. I have always been her reject. It has been like this for a very long time now. She is also very stubborn and not the type to ever admit she is wrong or apologize. I have tried apologizing even though I did nothing wrong to her, but she still will not budge even a little. Will the way she treated me affect how I treat my future kids? I think about my mom every day, and I don't want to ever make someone feel how she made me feel. My mother left me to pursue her career. I saw her once a week or twice a semester. I really needed to talk to someone about how much I missed her and how unhappy I was when she left me. My grandmother was my caregiver. She was an energetic carefree person throughout my childhood. She had raised me from the time I was a baby. She was always feisty and full of life, but she also had heart problems. In 2009 she started getting really sick again with her heart and was in and out of the hospital for most of the year. At one point we were told to prepare ourselves because she wouldn't live much longer. Sadly, she got worse and worse over the next couple of weeks, and before we knew it, palliative care was telling us that she would only have a couple of more months left. On November 18, 2011 at approximately 9:00 a.m. Eastern Standard Time, Fanny passed away. I loved my Fanny more than anything! She was the only person there for me when I needed someone. She understood my disability. We communicated to each other with our eyes. My dad also died from a massive heart attack. He smoked cigarettes all his life, and he had a midlife crisis and turned to drugs. No one knew this but me. I saw a white powdered substance hidden. I also had to learn that I could not assume any responsibility for my father's actions. He demonstrated that he was immature and irresponsible.

My father and mother were two very intelligent people, but their lives were a bit confusing. My mother has never been maternal, and I felt like she missed an important growing point in my life. This was over thirty years ago, and I never really forgave her 100 percent because anytime I talked to her about it in sign language or tried to explain the pain I was experiencing, I would always be ignored or shut down and told that I didn't know what I was talking about. She never wanted to discuss anything that had to do with emotions.

Every parent has a favorite child. I was always the underdog in my family because I was different. I can't remember if I was liked or disliked, or my darkest or happiest days. So in the back of my head I've always shown her love by providing financial and with material things. However, what I really wanted the most is love from her and to be understood. Growing up as a teenager, I felt the need to get out and find peace.

I often visit my deaf friends because they assist me with emotional support, love, and respect. My friends' parents always seem to understand what we're talking about, and they are baffled when I explain the drama in my life. They were so baffled that they exploded. When I have family differences, I may bring up facts. When I submit the truth, she will be irate and tell me how I make stuff up and I always think someone is out to get me. I didn't understand why she would say this to me. She's the only family member I have relationship problems with. I've never had friends or had anyone approach me that way my whole life. I never expect someone close to my heart to say anything would abuse my character. However, despite all these flaws, I need to find some redeeming characteristic to facilitate this relationship.

I know hate is a strong word, but I think about how I describe my mother's feelings toward me growing up the only dysfunctional child in my family.

My family has difficulties with intimacy, forming close relationships, and dread letting go of a relationship, even when it's destructive. They may be out of touch with their feelings and their spirituality and lack a sense of meaning in their lives. My deficient family. I have been hurt more by omission than by commission. Frequently, my physical impairment contributes to parental inadequacy. As a child I had to take on adult responsibilities because no one knew how to speak sign language. There was no help to guide me forward in the right direction. I'm a dysfunctional child. I experienced trauma and pain from my family's actions, words, and attitudes. Because of this trauma I experienced, I grew up changed, different from other children. I had to prepare myself for adulthood because I was forced into unnatural roles within my family. For some of my dysfunctional friends, this led them to flee their pain by alcohol or drug use because of the neglect and family abuse they had to face.

I tried hard to build my relationship with my family. I was tired of being in some instances strained and unnatural. Usually there's always one in every family who has a serious problem that would impact every other family member. However, I always felt I was the lost child because I was isolated. I felt like an outsider in the family being ignored by parents and siblings. Now let's stop here for just a moment. I just used the word *dysfunction*. Please understand what this term means before you shut it out. No one wants this term attached to them. Dysfunctional families are the stuff of psychiatrists and situational comedies, or so we've been conditioned to believe. Many don't want to admit there is some level of struggle in all families, all marriages, all relationships.

My parents always had these big ambitions for me. They told me what my career should be, who my friends should be, what kind of car I should drive, and who I should date or marry. It's like they expected me to be perfect but didn't really believe I could blow my nose. I felt like I was suffocating, but if I got the least bit independent, they tried to control me with money.

When I met my husband, I got that little maternal instinct tug on the heartstring, and I definitely saw us having children once we got settled in a bit and got our jobs established. However, as our marriage was taking off, I started to realize just how dysfunctional my own family really was. I finally found freedom and independence, and the more independent I became, the more tension there was with my family.

When I finally began to face these issues head on, I started seeing all sorts of emotional abuse, both in my recent history and in my childhood. With my mother being unwilling to talk about the issues, I finally made a decision to "separate" from her. As I continue sorting through the issues and healing emotionally, I find myself once again completely averse to starting a family.

When I think about all the issues and scars I carry, I can't imagine being able to hold myself together at times, much less care for a child. When I think about all the money I spend on fixing myself, I can't imagine having such a huge financial responsibility. I think about how much my family hurt me and how terrible it must be for your oldest child to abandon you to be with another family. As for me, that wasn't a good feeling.

Now I realize that by learning from my experience, it is unlikely that the cycle will repeat. In fact, I would make it a personal mission to make sure it didn't happen. In any case, I am terrified of the possibility. My parents never wanted me, as a child with disability. It was an unexpected, unplanned, and unwanted birth. My parents grew to love me despite my disability.

I came from a very dysfunctional family, and yes, I have children. Before I had my first child, I wondered all the time if I should have a kid, and if I did, would they have a mental disorder like those who were close to my heart? I waited until eighteen and a half to have my first child, and as soon as I found out I was pregnant, nothing else mattered. I wanted that baby very much. I was going to be the best mom I could possibly be. Then I had my second daughter, but she didn't live. My first husband cleaned out his closet and left us. Shortly after I found out my youngest daughter had autism. If I could go back and do it all again, you know what? I would love my daughter even with all the things we have to face every day, and I am not the best mother in the world, but I sure do try. If my children ever need me, unlike my parents, I will be there every time. I do not know if this helps. Everyone's life is different, but that was my life before and after.

ABOUT THE AUTHOR

Henry Smith is the founder of H.F. Enterprise, a positioning and branding firm that help consultants the deaf and disabled and others thought his leadership, he speaks to organizations on topics such as getting intimate with the deaf community, leadership, Visually impairment and independence. He was born in Newport News, Virginia. He has always enjoyed reading but wasn't satisfied with the literature that was being written for abuse deaf children and young adults, which influenced him to write Novels like "A Moment of Silence."

CPSIA information can be obtained
at www.ICGtesting.com
Printed in the USA
BVHW082051220819
556531BV00009B/787/P

9 780228 809715